G

for My Day

READ • TRUST • BELIEVE

ISBN: 978-1-963492-07-1

Assembled and Produced for Life Outreach International by
Breakfast for Seven
breakfastforseven.com

Printed in the United States of America.

Introduction

God's Word for My Day is a unique devotional featuring a daily Scripture, a quick inspirational thought and a designated space for you to journal your thoughts and prayers as you hear God's voice each day.

Divided into four editions – winter, spring, summer and fall – this devotional will encourage you in your faith and help you grow in your relationship with the Lord as you read through the Bible. By journaling your thoughts and listening for God's voice, you are activating, trusting and believing His Word!

READ

TRUST

BELIEVE

December 1

*Lord, how wonderful you are! You have stored up
so many good things for us, like a treasure chest
heaped up and spilling over with blessings—all
for those who honor and worship you! Everybody
knows what you can do for those who turn and hide
themselves in you.* (Psalm 31:19 TPT)

God has a treasure chest in heaven for you that He put there long, long ago. He immediately started filling it with blessings, and then He kept filling it! Every time He thinks about you and His love for you, He adds another blessing so that it is *heaped up and spilling over* with blessings for you. And He's not going to stop! He just keeps piling those blessings on! How great is His love for you! Stretch out your hands to the Lord today. Ask and receive the good things He has stored up in heaven just for you.

_____

_____

_____

_____

_____

_____

_____

_____

_____

_____

December 2

If things aren't going well for you, ask yourself: *How is my heart?* Solomon says that the heart affects *all that you are,* and from it *flows the wellspring of life.* If you are worn out, what are you giving your heart to that you shouldn't be? If you are confused, whose thoughts — besides God's — have you allowed into your heart? Guard yourself against any of these soul stealers. Listen carefully to your spirit. Pay attention to how you feel. Fill your thoughts with God and let Him fill your heart with His Spirit and give you life.

Lord, I believe . . .

_____

_____

_____

_____

_____

_____

_____

_____

_____

_____

December 3

YAHWEH is my best friend and my shepherd. I always have more than enough. (Psalm 23:1 TPT)

It is so encouraging to know that the Lord is our best friend and Shepherd. A shepherd not only leads and guides his sheep, but he also provides food, shelter and protection. God cares for all your needs, even your need for rest and restoration. When life becomes chaotic and crazy, your Good Shepherd will bring you to a place of peace and calm. When you walk through a dark and difficult season, He'll walk with you, navigating the way. His attention and devotion to you is extravagant. You will never lack with Him. He cares for you! He loves you!

Lord, I believe . . .

December 4

> *If we confess our sins, he is faithful and just and will forgive us our sins and purify us from all unrighteousness.* (1 John 1:9)

You may find yourself carrying the weight of past sins today. The good news is that we are already forgiven because of Jesus's sacrifice. We were forgiven the moment He died on the cross. When this verse says to *confess our sins*, it doesn't mean to ask for forgiveness – we've already received forgiveness. We are told simply to call our sin what it is and confess it to God. Acknowledging our sins will only bring us closer to Him.

Lord, I believe . . .

December 5

For we brought nothing into the world, and we can take nothing out of it. (1 Timothy 6:7)

The fullness of life comes through knowing God; it is only through Jesus that we are made whole and complete. A lot of times people think that if only they had more money or more possessions that they would be happier or more content, but time and time again this fails. Remember that the Lord will meet your every need. Simply trust in Him and His will for your life, and you will feel the fullness and contentment that comes from being in His presence.

Lord, I believe . . .

_____
_____
_____
_____
_____
_____
_____
_____
_____
_____
_____
_____
_____
_____
_____

December 6

> *There is no fear in love. But perfect love drives out fear, because fear has to do with punishment. The one who fears is not made perfect in love.* (1 John 4:18)

We are told in Scripture that God is love – His whole being is love and that love is poured out onto all of us. The more you commune with God and embrace the love He freely gives, the less fear you will have in your life. God's perfect love drives out any fears or anxieties that may be holding you back. What do you fear most? Know that God is bigger than that fear, and His love is great enough to cover all fear today.

Lord, I believe . .

_____

_____

_____

_____

_____

_____

_____

_____

_____

_____

_____

_____

_____

_____

December 7

For the word of God is alive and active. Sharper than any double-edged sword, it penetrates even to dividing soul and spirit, joints and marrow; it judges the thoughts and attitudes of the heart.

(Hebrews 4:12)

Where do you turn in times of difficulty? In times of joy? We are told that the Word of God is active and alive. Ultimately, there is no good place to turn in any situation except to God and His Word. It is powerful and active, able to work in your life and in any situation you may be going through. Challenge yourself to turn to the Word today and allow its power to work in your life through any situation you may be facing.

Lord, I believe . . .

_____

_____

_____

_____

_____

_____

_____

_____

_____

_____

_____

December 8

> **Jesus, the Anointed One, is always the same—
> yesterday, today, and forever.** (Hebrews 13:8 TPT)

Jesus is the same today as He was in the Gospel stories in Matthew, Mark, Luke and John. He is the same today as He was when God created the world. He will be the same in the future when He returns to the earth. His love is unchanging. His mercy is unchanging. His grace is unchanging. You can trust Him to be who He says He will be and do what His Word says He will do.

Lord, I believe . . .

_____

_____

_____

_____

_____

_____

_____

_____

_____

_____

_____

_____

_____

_____

> *Above all, set yourself apart as a model of a life nobly lived. With dignity, demonstrate integrity in all that you teach.* (Titus 2:7 TPT)

Have you ever heard someone say, "Do as I say, not as I do"? Unfortunately, our lives don't always reflect the integrity that we may challenge others to live up to. But a solid understanding of God's Word can lead us to live godly lives. Paul challenges Titus to model right living and demonstrate right believing – in other words, to practice what you preach. According to Titus 2, this kind of living makes you a walking advertisement for God's goodness and grace.

Lord, I believe . . .

_____

_____

_____

_____

_____

_____

_____

_____

_____

_____

_____

_____

December 10

> *The men were amazed and asked, "What kind
> of man is this? Even the winds and the waves
> obey him!"* (Matthew 8:27)

Even the winds and the waves obey our Lord, but there is so much more to our all-powerful Father. He created the earth and has command over His domain. He causes the seasons to change and the rain to fall from the sky. He created you in His image, and you, too, are called to obey the Father. Look to Him for guidance and earnestly ask Him for direction today.

Lord, I believe . . .

_____
_____
_____
_____
_____
_____
_____
_____
_____
_____
_____
_____
_____
_____
_____
_____

"*If you build your life on biblical principles, you will find the positive effects, benefits and blessings to be undeniable.*"

James Robison

READ

TRUST

BELIEVE

December 11

Now the LORD was gracious to Sarah as he had said, and the LORD did for Sarah what he had promised. (Genesis 21:1)

After decades of trying to conceive, Sarah was 90 years old when she gave birth to her first child. It may not have been the timing that Sarah wanted, but it was in God's perfect plan. What have you been praying for to be delivered in your life? Whatever it is, don't lose faith! God's timing is perfect, and He keeps His promises.

Lord, I believe . . .

_____

_____

_____

_____

_____

_____

_____

_____

_____

_____

_____

_____

_____

_____

December 12

> *"The fire on the altar must be kept burning; it must not go out. Every morning the priest is to add firewood and arrange the burnt offering on the fire and burn the fat of the fellowship offerings on it. The fire must be kept burning on the altar continuously; it must not go out."* (Leviticus 6:12-13)

Just as the Levites had daily offerings to burn, we, too, should come to God each day in worship and thankfulness. Humbling ourselves before Him reminds us that He is God, and we are not. Rejoice in the fact our Father always has a listening ear and isn't there to judge or condemn us, but rather to offer peace and comfort.

Lord, I believe . . .

_____

_____

_____

_____

_____

_____

_____

_____

_____

_____

_____

_____

December 13

And consider the example that Jesus, the Anointed One, has set before us. Let his mindset become your motivation. (Philippians 2:5 TPT)

Jesus's mindset was authentic humility. He approached life with a servant's heart, not a selfish attitude. If any one person deserved to be worshipped, it was the Man, Jesus; yet He was the One who knelt down and washed the feet of His disciples. He was the One who reached out and touched the untouchable, making them clean. He was the One who broke the Sabbath laws so that a person wouldn't have to suffer another day before receiving their healing. When His mindset is your motivation, you will put others first – not out of fear or self-degradation, but out of authentic love, humility and passion for Christ.

Lord, I believe . . .

_____

_____

_____

_____

_____

_____

_____

_____

_____

_____

December 14

> **No one should seek their own good,
> but the good of others.** (1 Corinthians 10:24)

What can you do today to intentionally seek the good of others? When was the last time you helped someone grow in their relationship with Jesus? We have freedom through Christ, yet we are called to lift up those around us, and sometimes that requires sacrifice. However, you will often find that when you sacrifice for the good of those around you, you will reap the fruit of that relationship and grow in your own relationship with Christ.

Lord, I believe . . .

_____
_____
_____
_____
_____
_____
_____
_____
_____
_____
_____
_____
_____
_____

Then Jesus said to her, "Daughter, because you dared to believe, your faith has healed you. Go with peace in your heart and be free from your suffering!"
(Mark 5:34 TPT)

A woman who had been bleeding for twelve years dared to believe that being close enough to touch Jesus would heal her. A father whose daughter was near death dared to believe that, in a crowd of people all wanting their own healing, Jesus would hear his plea and save his daughter. Hannah, Abraham, Peter, Paul, Esther, Job . . . the list goes on and on of people in the Bible who dared to believe that God was who He said He was and would do what He said He would do. And God did not let a single one of them down. What are you daring to believe Jesus for in your own life?

Lord, I believe . . .

_____

_____

_____

_____

_____

_____

_____

_____

_____

_____

> *But the wisdom from above is always pure, filled with peace, considerate and teachable. It is filled with love and never displays prejudice or hypocrisy in any form.* (James 3:17 TPT)

James describes two types of wisdom: worldly wisdom and heavenly wisdom. Worldly wisdom is selfish, jealous, proud and divisive. It assumes it knows everything. Heavenly wisdom is pure and full of peace, love, kindness and respect. It is teachable and open to correction. Pray for God to give you wisdom that produces peace and is pure of heart. Seek wise counsel. When gaining counsel, follow wisdom that leads to peace because peace is from God.

Lord, I believe . . .

_____

_____

_____

_____

_____

_____

_____

_____

_____

_____

_____

_____

December 17

*Is it proper for us to sin, just so good things
may come? May it never be! Yet there are some
who slander us and claim that is what we teach.
They deserve to be condemned for even saying it!*
(Romans 3:8 TPT)

Jesus died to cover a multitude of sins, and God forgives sin. The Bible tells us to forgive so we will be forgiven. But forgiveness is not a license to sin! When God truly enters your heart, you want to please Him. Stay away from teaching that gives license to sin. Though grace does abound, it is not to be abused. Run to grace and remain under the shadow of the Almighty.

Lord, I believe . . .

December 18

> **To this end I strenuously contend with all the energy
> Christ so powerfully works in me.** (Colossians 1:29)

Paul gives full credit to Christ from whom he draws his strength. When we acknowledge the working power and strength of God in our lives, so much can be accomplished for His Kingdom. Even in his last days, Paul was fervently working for the glory of God, continually acknowledging and thanking Christ for His energy and power at work!

Lord, I believe . . .

_____

_____

_____

_____

_____

_____

_____

_____

_____

_____

_____

_____

_____

_____

_____

December 19

> *"So I give you now a new commandment: Love each other just as much as I have loved you. For when you demonstrate the same love I have for you by loving one another, everyone will know that you're my true followers."* (John 13:34-35 TPT)

Jesus emphasized this teaching of love to His disciples, especially in the book of John. Often, we miss out on what's important because it seems so simple, so ordinary, so "I've heard this all before." Jesus tells the disciples to love one another just as He loved them. The way they chose to love is how people would know they were Christ-followers. The same is still true for us today. Don't miss the message because you've heard it before. Love — that is the way of the Gospel.

Lord, I believe . . .

_____

_____

_____

_____

_____

_____

_____

_____

_____

_____

> *Speak up for those who cannot speak for themselves, for the rights of all who are destitute. Speak up and judge fairly; defend the rights of the poor and needy.* (Proverbs 31:8-9)

We are called to speak for those who cannot speak for themselves. We live in a world where many people are voiceless against corruption and power. Do you have a voice in places that others do not? How can you use your voice today to defend the rights of others? Act with love on behalf of people who need a helping hand.

Lord, I believe . . .

_____

_____

_____

_____

_____

_____

_____

_____

_____

_____

_____

_____

_____

_____

"God doesn't expect what He does in our lives to be kept secret; He wants people to know the difference He can make."

Betty Robison

READ

TRUST

BELIEVE

*Then Jesus told his disciples a parable to show them
that they should always pray and not give up.*
(Luke 18:1)

Pray, pray and pray some more. If an unjust judge can change his mind, surely our God, a God of justice, is hearing our prayers. Like the widow coming to the unjust judge, we are to persist in our faith and not lose heart as we pray without giving up. Pray today until you can thank Him for the answer – even if you don't receive the answer right away, have full faith in Him that He will reveal all to you in His perfect timing.

Lord, I believe . . .

_____
_____
_____
_____
_____
_____
_____
_____
_____
_____
_____
_____
_____

December 22

> **On the contrary, we speak as those approved by God to be entrusted with the gospel. We are not trying to please people but God, who tests our hearts.** (1 Thessalonians 2:4)

We shouldn't live to please anyone but God. It is so easy to become wrapped up in what others think and feel about us, but, ultimately, we live to please the Lord. We have been entrusted with the Gospel, and we are called as His chosen people to share it. This pleases God. You may find that some people don't like what you have to say about the Gospel, but God has a plan for each person, and you are planting seeds in lives around you when you speak as someone approved and entrusted with the Gospel.

Lord, I believe . . .

_____

_____

_____

_____

_____

_____

_____

_____

_____

_____

_____

December 23

Who could ever wrap their minds around the riches of God, the depth of his wisdom, and the marvel of his perfect knowledge? Who could ever explain the wonder of his decisions or search out the mysterious way he carries out his plans? (Romans 11:33 TPT)

What do you love most about God? Make a list of all the things you love about Him. He is so abundantly good. He loves us with a perfect and amazing love. We will never be able to wrap our minds around the full riches of God here on earth. His glory is unmatchable. He is the Rock of Ages, the most Holy God. From Him and through Him and for Him are all things. Praise Him as the majestic God He is. To Him alone is the glory forever.

Lord, I believe . . .

_____

_____

_____

_____

_____

_____

_____

_____

_____

_____

_____

December 24

> *But I have this against you: you have abandoned
> the passionate love you had for me at the beginning.
> Think about how far you have fallen! Repent and
> do the works of love you did at first.*
>
> (Revelation 2:4-5TPT)

In this passage, Jesus is challenging the Church to renew their passion, repent of idolatry (which is putting other things before God) and go back to the *works of love* that they did when they first met Him. Sometimes we get so caught up in doing good that we lose sight of Who we're doing it for. When this happens, it's important to go back to the basics — spend time with God, worship Him and talk with Him. When you do, your passion will ignite again.

Lord, I believe . . .

_____

_____

_____

_____

_____

_____

_____

_____

_____

_____

December 25

> **But give reverent honor in your hearts to the Anointed One and treat him as the holy Master of your lives. And if anyone asks about the hope living within you, always be ready to explain your faith.** (1 Peter 3:15 TPT)

Sharing your faith may seem intimidating. One way to make it not feel so intimidating is to focus on your love for Christ. A heart fully in love gushes about the object of its love. If anyone asks you about the hope living in you or why you follow Jesus, tell them what you love most about Him and what He has done for you. Your testimony is powerful because it is your own experience. Think about what drew you to God and start there. Then invite that person into any further discussions at their own pace.

Lord, I believe . . .

_____

_____

_____

_____

_____

_____

_____

_____

_____

_____

December 26

> **Consider him who endured such opposition from sinners, so that you will not grow weary and lose heart.** (Hebrews 12:3)

Your life is like a race, a path carved out by God on which you must run. You will encounter obstacles, stretches of time where you feel exhausted and other hindrances. However, we are called to persevere through those difficulties and run the race. Set your eyes on Jesus and recall all that He endured for you today – let that motivate you to push through the tough spots and avoid losing heart. He is cheering you on, running right alongside you!

Lord, I believe . . .

_____

_____

_____

_____

_____

_____

_____

_____

_____

_____

_____

_____

December 27

> *"They will be like a tree planted by the water that sends out its roots by the stream. It does not fear when heat comes; its leaves are always green. It has no worries in a year of drought and never fails to bear fruit."* (Jeremiah 17:8)

When we put our trust and confidence in the Lord, we flourish like the parable of the tree planted by the stream. We know that Jesus is living water, and when our roots drink from Him, we bear fruit. From where are your roots absorbing nutrients? Where are you placing your trust and confidence today? Turn to God and know that He is where we receive life!

Lord, I believe . . .

_____

_____

_____

_____

_____

_____

_____

_____

_____

_____

_____

_____

> *"For what use is it to gain all the wealth and power of this world, with everything it could offer you, at the cost of your own life? And what could be more valuable to you than your own soul?"*
>
> (Mark 8:36-37 TPT)

Studies have shown that there are common regrets of the dying. Many people regret having spent so much time at work. Others regret all the time wasted worrying about what others thought or living the life that others wanted rather than being true to oneself. Some regret not traveling more, losing touch with friends, not taking better care of their health, not spending more time with their kids, being too serious and not having enough fun in life and not having the courage to be themselves. The Bible encourages us not to lose our lives in the pursuit of wealth or power. Pursue the Lord first in all things and not the things of the world.

Lord, I believe . . .

_____

_____

_____

_____

_____

_____

_____

_____

December 29

So if you know of an opportunity to do the right thing today, yet you refrain from doing it, you're guilty of sin. (James 4:17 TPT)

James says that if you are given the opportunity to do the right thing and you procrastinate, that is sin! It is rarely ever too late to do the right thing, but the best time to do the right thing is immediately. As you have opportunity today, do what you know is good and right. Do not hold back or wait until a perfect time or even until a more comfortable time. If you have opportunity today to do right, just do it. If you don't know what to do, do the last thing you felt the Lord tell you to do. Go back and complete that task, then return for the next.

Lord, I believe . . .

_____

_____

_____

_____

_____

_____

_____

_____

_____

_____

December 30

> *Then I will say to my soul, "Don't be discouraged; don't be disturbed, for I fully expect my Savior-God to break through for me. Then I'll have plenty of reasons to praise him all over again." Yes, he is my saving grace!* (Psalm 43:5 TPT)

We all have times when we need to be encouraged and reminded to put our hope in God again. The authors of Psalms 42 and 43 had to give themselves back-to-back pep talks. Psalm 42:11 and 43:5 say the exact same thing: *Don't be discouraged; don't be disturbed, for I fully expect my Savior-God to break through for me.* It's okay if you have to keep encouraging yourself. Don't give up on yourself, and don't give up on God. He will come through for you and give you reasons to praise!

Lord, I believe . . .

_____

_____

_____

_____

_____

_____

_____

_____

_____

_____

Whatever this year holds, secure yourself in God's Word. Believe what He says above anything you hear in the news. Anchor your soul to His eternal promises."

Randy Robison

READ

TRUST

BELIEVE

December 31

*"I give them eternal life, and they shall never perish;
no one will snatch them out of my hand. My Father,
who has given them to me, is greater than all; no
one can snatch them out of my Father's hand."*
(John 10:28-29)

God is bigger and stronger than any adversity that may come against you today or any day. Rest in the comfort of knowing that you are held in the palm of the Father's hand and no powers of darkness are strong enough to pull you away from that. Nothing will ever compare to being in the presence of your Father and feeling the confidence of having Him on your side.

Lord, I believe . . .

_____

_____

_____

_____

_____

_____

_____

_____

_____

_____

_____

_____

January 1

> *Create in me a pure heart, O God, and renew a steadfast spirit within me.* (Psalm 51:10)

This psalm could easily be something you pray every morning. Do you ever feel like you've entered a day and nothing feels quite right? Pray that God creates a pure heart and renews a steadfast spirit in you. These two things will get you through anything with a supernatural peace and feeling of fulfillment that cannot be found except for in the hands of the Father.

Lord, I believe . . .

January 2

> *". . . I will go to the king, even though it is against the law. And if I perish, I perish."*
> (Esther 4:16)

Although an extreme circumstance, in this verse, Esther embodies the fearless faith that Christ calls us to. What situations has God called you to that you've turned away from because you were afraid of the unknown? Something as simple as sharing your faith with a nonbeliever can bring upon feelings of doubt and anxiety, but let this serve as a reminder that with God on your side you have nothing to fear!

Lord, I believe . . .

_____

_____

_____

_____

_____

_____

_____

_____

_____

_____

_____

_____

_____

_____

> *Then we will no longer be infants, tossed back and forth by the waves, and blown here and there by every wind of teaching and by the cunning and craftiness of people in their deceitful scheming.*
>
> (Ephesians 4:14)

As believers, we must be grounded in God's Word. The Enemy is constantly seeking to derail our walks with God and keep us from maturing spiritually. On earth, we will constantly face temptation, but remember the Spirit of Christ that lives within us. We know the truth, and although he may try again and again, the Devil will never win. Speak that truth over yourself today!

Lord, I believe . . .

_____

_____

_____

_____

_____

_____

_____

_____

_____

_____

_____

_____

January 4

> *"What no eye has seen, what no ear has heard, and what no human mind has conceived"—the things God has prepared for those who love him. . . .*
>
> (1 Corinthians 2:9)

The things God has prepared for us are so far from this world that we cannot imagine them! No human mind has conceived what He has in store for us. It can be difficult to fathom the amount of love the Father has for His disobedient and sinful children; yet He has prepared great things for you. His love is unending, unfailing and unconditional! What a great blessing.

Lord, I believe . . .

_____

_____

_____

_____

_____

_____

_____

_____

_____

_____

_____

_____

January 5

Give us this day our daily bread – this is the spiritual sustenance that Jesus is talking about when His disciples tell Him to eat. Our real food is the spiritual nourishment we receive from our Father that helps us to grow and mature. He freely shares this with us and is constantly feeding us through His Word. Ask God for your daily bread today and be filled with it!

Lord, I believe . . .

_____

_____

_____

_____

_____

_____

_____

_____

_____

_____

_____

_____

_____

_____

_____

January 6

Still others, like seed sown among thorns, hear the word; but the worries of this life, the deceitfulness of wealth and the desires for other things come in and choke the word, making it unfruitful.
(Mark 4:18-19)

The parable of the sower teaches us about the importance of our environments. So many factors can interfere with the successful growth of a seed. When we sow seed into the lives of others, it may not be as successful as we hope because of the state of the soil and its environment. In the same way, our environments can inhibit our spiritual growth. If you're not seeing growth, look at your environment and ask God to show you what is inhibiting growth in your life.

Lord, I believe . . .

_____

_____

_____

_____

_____

_____

_____

_____

_____

_____

> He went on: "What comes out of a person is what defiles them. For it is from within, out of a person's heart, that evil thoughts come. . . ." (Mark 7:20-21)

Jesus is speaking to the Pharisees about the danger of holding on to their traditions. He says that their hearts are far from Him. Instead of worrying about adhering to their traditions, He urges them to be concerned about their hearts. In doing so, Jesus showed them what was truly important: the state of their hearts. The Pharisees never quite understood that their obsession with rules and law was what pulled their hearts away from Jesus. It is a dangerous way to live! Are you more concerned with rules and religious tradition than the state of your heart?

Lord, I believe . . .

_____

_____

_____

_____

_____

_____

_____

_____

_____

_____

_____

January 8

But while Joseph was there in the prison, the LORD was with him; he showed him kindness and granted him favor in the eyes of the prison warden. (Genesis 39:20-21)

No matter our present circumstances, it's important to stop and remember that our Father is with us in the peaks and the valleys. Just as He never left Joseph's side, He will surely never leave yours. Refresh your spirit in this truth today and know that He is with you always.

Lord, I believe . . .

_____
_____
_____
_____
_____
_____
_____
_____
_____
_____
_____
_____
_____
_____

January 9

> *We can demolish every deceptive fantasy that opposes God and break through every arrogant attitude that is raised up in defiance of the true knowledge of God. We capture, like prisoners of war, every thought and insist that it bow in obedience to the Anointed One.* (2 Corinthians 10:5 TPT)

Do you ever feel like there is a war going on in your mind? Try as you might to hold on to your faith and confidence in God's plan for your life, doubts, insecurities, shame and fear can creep their way into your thinking. That's because you are in a war! Only, the weapons you fight with are not physical, but spiritual. The Devil wants to strong-arm you into believing you cannot make it; but the sword of the Spirit, which is the Word of God, says, *I [you] can do all things through Christ who strengthens me [you]* (Philippians 4:13 NKJV). Be intentional today – take every thought captive that does not line up with Scripture.

Lord, I believe . . .

_____

_____

_____

_____

_____

_____

_____

"The only One who can comfort and heal a broken heart is the Father. When we realize how much He loves us, we can be a channel for His love."

James Robison

READ

TRUST

BELIEVE

January 10

I'm writing to encourage you to fan into a flame and rekindle the fire of the spiritual gift God imparted to you when I laid my hands upon you. For God will never give you the spirit of fear, but the Holy Spirit who gives you mighty power, love, and self-control.

(2 Timothy 1:6-7 TPT)

God has given spiritual gifts to every believer. Spiritual gifts that lie dormant in our lives are no different than something tucked away and not used. Paul challenges Timothy – and us! – to awaken the gifts that have been imparted to us by the Holy Spirit. These gifts give us the revelation of light to know His will, love to motivate us to do His will and power to carry it out.

Lord, I believe . . .

January 11

> *As we enter into God's faith-rest life we cease from our own works, just as God celebrates his finished works and rests in them.* (Hebrews 4:10 TPT)

Of all the commandments that God has ever given, we seem to have the hardest time with honoring the Sabbath. If God took a day to rest, surely we can too! The Sabbath is both a gift of rest to us and a challenge to trust in God. By abstaining from work one day of the week, we are telling God that we trust Him to help us accomplish all we need to do on the other six days. When you enter *God's faith-rest life*, you are inviting God to be your strength. Put the Sabbath to the test. Take the day off. Enjoy a day of relaxation and rest and see if you aren't refreshed and ready for the challenges of the work week.

Lord, I believe . . .

_____

_____

_____

_____

_____

_____

_____

_____

_____

_____

January 12

Let the morning bring me word of your unfailing love, for I have put my trust in you. Show me the way I should go, for to you I entrust my life.
(Psalm 143:8)

Remember this morning, and every morning, to put your trust in the Lord and His unfailing love. Trust that He will make your path clear as you entrust your life to Him. His love will never fail you – believe that today!

Lord, I believe . . .

_____

_____

_____

_____

_____

_____

_____

_____

_____

_____

_____

_____

_____

_____

_____

_____

January 13

> *Not only so, but we also glory in our sufferings, because we know that suffering produces perseverance; perseverance, character; and character, hope.* (Romans 5:3-4)

Remaining positive and even joyful through sufferings can be a difficult task; however, Paul writes that we must glory and rejoice in our sufferings because it produces perseverance, character and hope. When suffering produces hope, it builds confidence in a God who loves us. God is big enough to cover anything you are facing today. Let any negative feelings be transformed into perseverance, character and hope. Know that God loves you, train your mind to turn to Him through your suffering and rejoice that it is building up a greater purpose within you.

Lord, I believe . . .

_____
_____
_____
_____
_____
_____
_____
_____
_____
_____

January 14

As a result of our ministry, you are living letters written by Christ, not with ink but by the Spirit of the living God—not carved onto stone tablets but on the tablets of tender hearts. (2 Corinthians 3:3 TPT)

Have you ever asked someone to write you a letter of recommendation? The purpose of that letter is for someone else to validate your ability to do whatever it is you are applying to do, whether it be a job opportunity or adopting a child or receiving a scholarship or grant. In this passage, Paul says that the Corinthian people were his letter of recommendation, proving that he was a valid minister of the Gospel. Likewise, we are walking and talking *living letters written by Christ.*

Lord, I believe . . .

_____

_____

_____

_____

_____

_____

_____

_____

_____

_____

_____

January 15

> **Those who live to bless others will have blessings heaped upon them, and the one who pours out his life to pour out blessings will be saturated with favor.** (Proverbs 11:25 TPT)

In Israel, the Dead Sea is called *dead* because it has no outlet for fresh water to pour out. As water enters from the Jordan River, it gets stuck in the Dead Sea and never leaves. This could be a picture of greed versus generosity. A person with a greedy spirit wants to keep everything to themselves, because they fear that there isn't more where that came from. A person with a generous spirit, however, sees themselves as an open vessel; receiving and giving is a continuous cycle that keeps them healthy and alive. *Generosity brings prosperity* (v. 24) in God's economy!

Lord, I believe . . .

_____

_____

_____

_____

_____

_____

_____

_____

_____

_____

_____

January 16

> *"A thief has only one thing in mind—he wants to steal, slaughter, and destroy. But I have come to give you everything in abundance, more than you expect—life in its fullness until you overflow!"* (John 10:10 TPT)

God never does anything halfway. He pours out His blessings in abundance. When He fed the five thousand with two fish and five loaves of bread, they had twelve baskets of food leftover! If you want a cup of water, He'll give you a well that never runs dry. If you want to know love, He laid down His life for you. If you need peace, He'll give you a peace that is beyond comprehension. God always goes above and beyond. He never grows tired of doing good or providing for your needs!

Lord, I believe . . .

_____

_____

_____

_____

_____

_____

_____

_____

_____

_____

_____

January 17

> *What shall we conclude then? Do we have any advantage? Not at all! For we have already made the charge that Jews and Gentiles alike are all under the power of sin.* (Romans 3:9)

Comparison can be such a dangerous habit to give in to. You may find yourself comparing your sin with the sins of those around you. Instead, we should use God's standards as a guideline to compare our actions with. Sin is sin, and all we need in this life is His love and grace. Every human falls short of His glory. Ask God to help you recognize your own sinfulness today and to give you a spirit that relies on Him and His guidance to direct you away from it.

Lord, I believe . . .

_____
_____
_____
_____
_____
_____
_____
_____
_____
_____
_____

Then the LORD God formed a man from the dust of the ground and breathed into his nostrils the breath of life, and the man became a living being.

(Genesis 2:7)

You are a God-breathed creation! The dust that makes up our earthly bodies is just dust. It is God's breath of life that makes us living beings. It is when we realize that we are alive because of God's Spirit within us that we live fully and abundantly! His Spirit within us is what turns our hearts back to God and enables us to act and speak from a heart full of love and grace.

Lord, I believe . . .

_____

_____

_____

_____

_____

_____

_____

_____

_____

_____

_____

_____

January 19

> **The seventh time the servant reported, "A cloud as small as a man's hand is rising from the sea."**
> (1 Kings 18:44)

Elijah has just shown the prophets of Baal that God is the one true God! He answers them by fire and the people repent, but Elijah knows that God has more for them. They have experienced years of drought, so Elijah prays that God will bring the rain. Elijah sends his servant seven times to look for a cloud, and at the sight of a small cloud, he knows that his prayers have been answered. God always has more in store for us than we know, and like Elijah, we must remain faithful in Him!

Lord, I believe . . .

_____

_____

_____

_____

_____

_____

_____

_____

_____

_____

_____

_____

"We don't have to be perfect to come before God. He is waiting for us, longing to show us how to break out of our individual prisons. He wants us free!"

———————————

Betty Robison

READ

TRUST

BELIEVE

January 20

For the glorious name of the Lord is blessed forever and ever. From sunrise-brilliance to sunset-beauty, lift up his praise from dawn to dusk! For he rules on high over the nations with a glory that outshines even the heavens. (Psalm 113:2-4TPT)

A sunrise is brilliant as it breaks apart the darkness of night with dawn's early light. Whatever darkness you may be in or are walking out of, know that the light of God's love will bring you through. A sunset is beautiful as it wraps up another day – another gift from the Almighty. Even though what you're going through might hurt right now, it doesn't have to end ugly. God can bring beauty to any situation. Sing His praises from dawn to dusk, brilliance to beauty, beginning to end.

Lord, I believe . . .

_____

_____

_____

_____

_____

_____

_____

_____

_____

_____

January 21

> *But Jesus is worthy to receive a much greater glory than Moses, for the one who builds a house deserves to be honored more than the house he builds. Every house is built by someone, but God is the Designer and Builder of all things.* (Hebrews 3:3-4 TPT)

We must be careful not to worship created things over the Creator of all things. We can marvel at the stars in the sky, the diversity of human gifts, the beauty of nature, the taste of fresh fruit and the first signs of spring budding forth from the ground, but we must not worship those things. We can be grateful for loving relationships with our spouses, children, parents and friends, but we must not give them first place in our lives. We must remember that God created all things, and He gave us those relationships. He alone is worthy to be worshipped and praised!

Lord, I believe . . .

_____
_____
_____
_____
_____
_____
_____
_____
_____
_____

January 22

But the fruit of the Spirit is love, joy, peace, forbearance, kindness, goodness, faithfulness, gentleness and self-control. Against such things there is no law. (Galatians 5:22-23)

What fruit are you seeing in your life? The fruits of the Spirit are things we can look for and evaluate in our own lives. In our relationships with Christ, we are challenged to grow spiritually, and these fruits are evidence of that spiritual growth. Pray and ask God to help you to pull out any weeds that may be pulling good nutrients away from these important fruits.

Lord, I believe . . .

> *Do you not know that your bodies are temples of the Holy Spirit, who is in you, whom you have received from God? You are not your own; you were bought at a price. Therefore honor God with your bodies.* (1 Corinthians 6:19-20)

Jesus gave His body as a gift for us. Remember this as you honor God with your body. When you maintain your body, a gift you are given, it is a way to express gratitude, honor and praise to our Father. Are you treating your body as a temple that you are thankful for, or are you misusing it with poor eating habits and a lack of exercise?

Lord, I believe . . .

_____

_____

_____

_____

_____

_____

_____

_____

_____

_____

_____

_____

January 24

And without faith it is impossible to please God, because anyone who comes to him must believe that he exists and that he rewards those who earnestly seek him. (Hebrews 11:6)

Earnestly seeking God doesn't mean attempting to have a relationship with Him just by going to church every week. An earnest seeker devotes much time and energy to their belief in God. They are in frequent communication with the Father through prayer and worship. They seek Him in the world around them; they seek Him in His Word. How can you earnestly seek Him today?

Lord, I believe . . .

_____

_____

_____

_____

_____

_____

_____

_____

_____

_____

_____

_____

> *And before her twin sons were born, God spoke to Rebekah and said: "The oldest will serve the youngest." God spoke these words before the sons had done anything good or bad, which proves that God calls people not on the basis of their good or bad works, but according to his divine purpose.*
>
> (Romans 9:11-12 TPT)

Have you ever been jealous of what God has done in someone else's life? Resentment is a dangerous emotion. Resentment, if not confronted, can lead to bitterness and anger. The story of Jacob and Esau shows us that God does not make decisions based on our standards. A great antidote to resentment is gratitude. Thank the Lord for all He has done for you, and trust He knows what He is doing. God has a plan for your life that isn't dependent on what He is doing in someone else's.

Lord, I believe . . .

_____

_____

_____

_____

_____

_____

_____

_____

January 26

Show me your ways, LORD, teach me your paths.
(Psalm 25:4)

What path are you on? Is it one to which God has led you, or did you take a detour on an appealing path that distracted you? Your heart knows that God's path is always right. Ask God to guide you today; ask for confirmation that you are on His path or direction to return to it. As your Shepherd, God has promised to never leave you – He is there to guide you today and keep you on the right path.

Lord, I believe . . .

January 27

Have you ever wanted something so much that you could feel yourself salivating at the thought of possessing it? That is the longing that the sons of Korah describe in this psalm, the longing they had for the living God. They thirsted for God, like a deer panting for streams of water. That is a thirst that cannot be quenched except by the river's edge or the presence of God. Are you so passionate about God that you can literally feel yourself thirst for Him? Pray for that kind of passion! Pray for His presence in your life. Pray to know Him as the source of your satisfaction.

Lord, I believe . . .

_____

_____

_____

_____

_____

_____

_____

_____

_____

_____

_____

"We want you to carefully select from among yourselves seven godly men. Make sure they are honorable, full of the Holy Spirit and wisdom, and we will give them the responsibility of this crucial ministry of serving. That will enable us to give our full attention to prayer and preaching the word of God." (Acts 6:3-4 TPT)

The apostles were clear about God's mission for their lives: to preach the Word of God and make disciples of all the nations. This was a grand task, and the only way they would succeed was to stay focused on what God had called them to do. There are many important responsibilities in the world, but they are not all yours to carry. Be mindful to fulfill the task the Lord has given you, and don't worry about what someone else is doing.

Lord, I believe . . .

_____
_____
_____
_____
_____
_____
_____
_____
_____

January 29

> **"Rid yourselves of all the offenses you have committed, and get a new heart and a new spirit. Why will you die, people of Israel?"** (Ezekiel 18:31)

God doesn't like death! It is the punishment for sin, but we are blessed with an alternative option: we can repent and live! He offers us a new heart and a new spirit when we commit ourselves to Him and turn away from our old offenses. When we embrace this beautiful opportunity, our lives take on new meaning and purpose. We are living for the glory of the Father!

Lord, I believe . . .

_____
_____
_____
_____
_____
_____
_____
_____
_____
_____
_____
_____
_____
_____

"God wastes absolutely nothing – not even the messes we create from our own choices."

—————————

Tammy Trent

READ

TRUST

BELIEVE

January 30

A hot-tempered person stirs up conflict, but the one who is patient calms a quarrel. (Proverbs 15:18)

The Bible tells us that patience is important and useful. When we fix our eyes on Christ and look at the time Jesus spent on earth, we see the depiction of an extremely patient Shepherd. Patience requires self-control and a desire to please God. Pray for patience today. Pray that God will open your heart up to this trait and that you will reap the important benefits of a patient life.

Lord, I believe . . .

January 31

> *Keep your thoughts continually fixed on all that is authentic and real, honorable and admirable, beautiful and respectful, pure and holy, merciful and kind. And fasten your thoughts on every glorious work of God, praising him always.* (Philippians 4:8 TPT)

It's so easy for our minds to become cluttered with the busyness of life and all the responsibilities we have. This verse is such a great reminder to reset our thoughts each day. Try writing out each of the attributes listed in this verse on a piece of paper. Then each day when you wake up, before you start your day, take a moment to turn your thoughts toward God. Look over the list and ask God to help you keep those things at the forefront of your mind throughout the day. You'll be pleasantly surprised how your demeanor, outlook and countenance changes as you make this a daily practice.

Lord, I believe . . .

_____

_____

_____

_____

_____

_____

_____

_____

February 1

In him was life, and that life was the light of all mankind. The light shines in the darkness, and the darkness has not overcome it. (John 1:4-5)

Darkness has not, and will not, ever overcome the brilliant light that Jesus shines in this world. The Bible tells us how the story ends: He has already won, it is finished! We have reason to rejoice because the darkness has not overcome the light. We are guided by the heavenly light of our Father, and we, too, are called to be lights in the darkness of this world.

Lord, I believe . . .

_____

_____

_____

_____

_____

_____

_____

_____

_____

_____

_____

_____

_____

_____

February 2

> **So you are no longer a slave, but God's child; and since you are his child, God has made you also an heir.** (Galatians 4:7)

When Christ came, He brought a new covenant. With His sacrifice for our sin, we are no longer living under the law of the Old Testament. We are no longer slaves; we are free! You are a child of the Most High God! Being a child means being an heir, and your inheritance is an eternity with the Father in heaven – a place of perfect peace, joy and love.

Lord, I believe . . .

February 3

"You have not strengthened the weak or healed the sick or bound up the injured. You have not brought back the strays or searched for the lost. You have ruled them harshly and brutally." (Ezekiel 34:4)

Israel's leaders had not been good shepherds. They didn't search for the lost or bring back the strays; they didn't take care of the sick, weak or injured. They were leading the flock without the love and tenderness that our Shepherd leads us with. They were harsh and brutal. Do your actions reflect that of the Shepherd? Are you tender to your flock? Do you go after the lost and care for the sick?

Lord, I believe . . .

February 4

> *It's true that our freedom allows us to do anything,*
> *but that doesn't mean that everything we do is good*
> *for us. I'm free to do as I choose, but I choose to*
> *never be enslaved to anything.* (1 Corinthians 6:12 TPT)

Paul writes to the Galatians: *It is for freedom that Christ has set us free. Stand firm, then, and do not let yourselves be burdened again by a yoke of slavery* (Galatians 5:1). God values freedom so much that He gives us free will to *do anything, but that doesn't mean that everything we do is good for us.* You can become a slave to the things that you choose if you don't choose wisely. In both Paul's letter to the Corinthians and his letter to the Galatians, he encourages them to make choices that lead to life and freedom, because those are of God.

Lord, I believe . . .

_____

_____

_____

_____

_____

_____

_____

_____

_____

_____

February 5

**Cast your cares on the LORD and he will sustain
you; he will never let the righteous be shaken.**
(Psalm 55:22)

Have you ever felt shaken by your current circumstances? The Bible says that God will never let us be shaken. As long as we keep our hope in Him and trust that He cares for and sustains us, we will not be shaken by whatever we may face. He will not let you be shaken, but will you allow yourself to be shaken by things of this world? Cast your cares and worries and stress on God and trust that all will be taken care of through His strength.

Lord, I believe . . .

_____

_____

_____

_____

_____

_____

_____

_____

_____

_____

_____

_____

_____

February 6

> **Do not get drunk on wine, which leads to debauchery. Instead, be filled with the Spirit.**
> (Ephesians 5:18)

Open yourself to be filled with the Spirit today. When the Holy Spirit is in you, you are the whole and complete person He intends for you to be. Yield your heart and life to the Spirit; place your trust in God and His complete control over all areas of your life. God is waiting for you to choose Him and to invite His power and provision into all areas of your life.

Lord, I believe . . .

_____
_____
_____
_____
_____
_____
_____
_____
_____
_____
_____
_____
_____
_____

February 7

***I You must understand this at the outset:
Interpretation of scriptural prophecy requires
the Holy Spirit, for it does not originate from
someone's own imagination.*** (2 Peter 1:20 TPT)

God continues to speak today just as He did to the prophets.
Like a light in the darkness, He illuminates the Scriptures and
pierces our hearts with new revelations and understandings.
The Holy Spirit inspired the Scriptures, so it only makes sense
that we would need the Holy Spirit's help to interpret what He
wrote. Ask the Holy Spirit to give you understanding as you read
the Word today!

Lord, I believe . . .

February 8

> *To the fatherless he is a father. To the widow he is
> a champion friend. The lonely he makes part of a
> family. The prisoners he leads into prosperity until
> they sing for joy. This is our Holy God in his Holy
> Place! But for the rebels there is heartache
> and despair.* (Psalm 68:5-6 TPT)

God is everything you need. Orphaned? He is a parent to you.
Widowed? He is a friend to you. Lonely? He has the perfect family
in mind for you. Whether it be a father, friend or family – whatever
you need right now – He is the answer. You will never be satisfied
if you look to others to meet your needs. A life of joy awaits those
who trust in God and seek Him first.

Lord, I believe . . .

_____

_____

_____

_____

_____

_____

_____

_____

_____

_____

_____

"May God's Word be written in our hearts, not just carried in our hands."

James Robison

READ

TRUST

BELIEVE

February 9

See, your king comes to you, righteous and victorious, lowly and riding on a donkey, on a colt, the foal of a donkey. (Zechariah 9:9)

Christ our King did not come riding on a majestic horse, clad in armor or jewels. Christ came riding on a donkey – and not even an adult donkey, but a colt! What does this say about our Father and the image we are created in? Christ on a donkey is a picture of humility. We are not called to be wealthy or to stand out; we are called to humble ourselves.

Lord, I believe . . .

_____

_____

_____

_____

_____

_____

_____

_____

_____

_____

_____

_____

_____

_____

February 10

> *I pray that your partnership with us in the faith may*
> *be effective in deepening your understanding of every*
> *good thing we share for the sake of Christ.* (Philemon 1:6)

When you fellowship with the Lord and others in your community, sharing your faith and love toward Him and those around you, you will grow spiritually and develop a deeper understanding of the good that surrounds you. The partnership of faith will open your eyes and heart to the unceasing love that flows from heaven over you. We share in this goodness because of Christ!

Lord, I believe . . .

_____

_____

_____

_____

_____

_____

_____

_____

_____

_____

_____

_____

_____

GOD'S WORD FOR MY DAY — WINTER EDITION

February 11

> *"He has done this so that every person would long for God, feel their way to him, and find him—for he is the God who is easy to discover! It is through him that we live and function and have our identity; just as your own poets have said, 'Our lineage comes from him.'"* (Acts 17:27-28 TPT)

You may feel unknown to the world, but you can rest assured that you are known by God! We are all known by God, and God wants to be known by all. That's why He has made Himself *easy to discover*. He gives life and breath to all. He made the world and everything in it. He is ready to answer prayers and give salvation. He is not far from any one of us as we live and move and have our being in Him. His heart is that people would seek Him, reach out for Him and find Him.

Lord, I believe . . .

February 12

> *Peter shouted out, "Lord, if it's really you, then have me join you on the water!" "Come and join me," Jesus replied. So Peter stepped out onto the water and began to walk toward Jesus.*
>
> (Matthew 14:28-29 TPT)

In verse 27, Jesus shouted to the disciples from the top of the water He walked across: *"Be brave!"* And Peter responded by boldly asking Jesus to call him out onto the water with Him. Have you ever taken a leap of faith like Peter did that day? Jesus's offer to Peter is extended to you as well: *"Come and join Me."* Wherever Jesus is, we are always welcome. What is His voice calling you to do? Trust that whatever God calls you to is for your good. His plans for you are to prosper you and not to harm you, to give you a hope and a future (Jeremiah 29:11).

Lord, I believe . . .

_____

_____

_____

_____

_____

_____

_____

_____

_____

_____

February 13

> *But Herod both feared and stood in awe of John and kept him safely in custody, because he was convinced that he was a righteous and holy man. Every time Herod heard John speak, it disturbed his soul, but he was drawn to him and enjoyed listening to his words.* (Mark 6:20 TPT)

John the Baptist was known for speaking truth and declaring it boldly! John spoke directly to the mess that Herod had made when he married his brother's wife. Yet Herod was drawn to John and wanted to hear what he had to say. He was drawn to John even though he feared him. Even if a person's heart isn't right with God, hearing truth spoken in love will impact their soul. God can use this disruption to nudge people out of sin and invite them into the grace life. Speak the truth!

Lord, I believe . . .

_____

_____

_____

_____

_____

_____

_____

_____

_____

February 14

> *. . . may he work perfection into every part of you giving you all that you need to fulfill your destiny. And may he express through you all that is excellent and pleasing to him through your life-union with Jesus the Anointed One who is to receive all glory forever! Amen!* (Hebrews 13:21 TPT)

God has equipped you with everything you need to do His will. He will prepare you! His grace is sufficient, and His supply is enough. The key is to stay as close to Jesus as possible. Let the Word be a lamp to your feet and a light to your path. Return to Him for your daily bread. He will guide you with His eye upon you. That means you just keep your gaze fixed on Him and go where He says to go or move when He says to move. Remember always: He is the Good Shepherd.

Lord, I believe . . .

_____

_____

_____

_____

_____

_____

_____

_____

_____

February 15

Everyone comes naked from their mother's womb, and as everyone comes, so they depart. They take nothing from their toil that they can carry in their hands. (Ecclesiastes 5:15)

We enter the world with nothing, and we will leave this world with nothing. Pray that God opens your heart to His counsel concerning your wealth and belongings today. Ask how you can best steward your belongings in a way that brings honor and glory to Him. How can you best serve others and serve God with what you have been blessed with?

Lord, I believe . . .

> *"This is what the LORD Almighty said: 'Administer true justice; show mercy and compassion to one another.'"* (Zechariah 7:9)

God says that true justice is mercy and compassion. People are often quick to judge and reprimand others for their wrongdoings and shortcomings. When was the last time you showed mercy and compassion to those around you? Justice doesn't mean getting revenge or punishing someone; it means extending the unmerited grace of God to others even when you don't think they deserve it.

Lord, I believe . . .

_____

_____

_____

_____

_____

_____

_____

_____

_____

_____

_____

_____

_____

_____

February 17

God's marvelous grace has manifested in person, bringing salvation for everyone. This same grace teaches us how to live each day as we turn our backs on ungodliness and indulgent lifestyles, and it equips us to live self-controlled, upright, godly lives in this present age. (Titus 2:11-12 TPT)

Jesus is the manifestation of God's grace. That grace brought salvation to all who believe, but it also has a practical implications for our everyday lives. Grace teaches us how to live our lives unto the Lord. It enables us to turn our backs on what is ungodly and helps us step forward into a life of righteousness. Grace empowers us to have self-control. Today, if you're struggling to say no to sin, remember that you have Jesus living inside you and His grace will enable you to say yes to a life devoted to Him.

Lord, I believe . . .

_____

_____

_____

_____

_____

_____

_____

_____

_____

February 18

> *Discover creative ways to encourage others and to motivate them toward acts of compassion, doing beautiful works as expressions of love.*
>
> (Hebrews 10:24 TPT)

Make a list of all the possible ways you might encourage others. Be as creative as you wish. Maybe it's paying for someone's meal or coffee, sending a card, smiling and opening doors for strangers or saying thank you. Include the less obvious ideas too, the ones that seem random, the ones that make you say, "Holy Spirit, You want me to do *what?*" Include the things that others have done to encourage you. Once you have your list, go into the world and start spreading kindness to everyone you meet, doing beautiful works as expressions of love.

Lord, I believe . . .

_____

_____

_____

_____

_____

_____

_____

_____

_____

_____

"Every new anxiety brings us opportunity. We can either grow in our faith or we can give in to anxiety and become more miserable."

Randy Robison

READ

TRUST

BELIEVE

February 19

"Whoever does God's will is my brother and sister and mother." (Mark 3:35)

When we enter a relationship with God, we become heavenly family! You may be feeling lonely, unimportant or uncared for, but the truth is that you are surrounded by members of your heavenly family. Through Jesus, we gain new brothers and sisters and mothers. Are you actively part of a group of believers? When you spend time with your heavenly family your life will be enriched!

Lord, I believe . . .

_____
_____
_____
_____
_____
_____
_____
_____
_____
_____
_____
_____
_____
_____
_____
_____

February 20

> *No temptation has overtaken you except what is common to mankind. And God is faithful; he will not let you be tempted beyond what you can bear. But when you are tempted, he will also provide a way out so that you can endure it.* (1 Corinthians 10:13)

God is faithful and will always provide a means of escape from any temptation that you face. We are sure to face temptations of many kinds in our lifetimes, but because of the power of God, we have the strength to stand strong against temptation. Pray today that God opens your eyes to see His provided escape from any temptation that you may be facing.

Lord, I believe . . .

_____

_____

_____

_____

_____

_____

_____

_____

_____

_____

_____

_____

February 21

*"For the Son of Man came to seek and
to save the lost."* (Luke 19:10)

Jesus came to earth and touched the lives of people society disowned – the disfigured, the sick, the poor and those with unfavorable jobs. Jesus extended His love and compassion to all and left us with a message that said, *Even when others tell you that you don't belong, you will always have a place in My Kingdom.* Are you seeking the lost like Jesus did?

Lord, I believe . . .

_____

_____

_____

_____

_____

_____

_____

_____

_____

_____

_____

_____

_____

_____

_____

_____

> *After the earthquake came a fire, but the LORD*
> *was not in the fire. And after the fire came*
> *a gentle whisper.* (1 Kings 19:12)

God does not always work in the ways we want or expect Him to. Often times we wait in anticipation to hear from the Lord but fail to hear Him because He is not speaking to us in the ways we expect Him to. His Word doesn't always come in an earthquake or a fire; sometimes it comes in a gentle whisper. If you're waiting to hear from the Lord today, ask yourself how well you are listening.

Lord, I believe . . .

_____

_____

_____

_____

_____

_____

_____

_____

_____

_____

_____

_____

_____

_____

_____

February 23

This is love: He loved us long before we loved him. It was his love, not ours. He proved it by sending his Son to be the pleasing sacrificial offering to take away our sins. (1 John 4:10 TPT)

God said "I love you" first, knowing that not everyone would say it back. Some have reciprocated that love, but others may never say it back, and still more need time until they are ready. But God's love isn't dependent on our responses. He loves us, even when we don't love Him in return. God's love is who He is, and He will never stop loving us – no matter what we do, whether we reciprocate or not, because He loved us first.

Lord, I believe . . .

_____

_____

_____

_____

_____

_____

_____

_____

_____

_____

_____

_____

February 24

> **The world and its desires pass away, but whoever
> does the will of God lives forever.** (1 John 2:17)

Where are you placing your trust and confidence today? What desires have you acted on recently? Have your actions brought you closer to God? The things of this world will not last; the Bible says that the world will fade away. Place your trust in the Lord and set your eyes on the eternity that you have to look forward to. When your actions are motivated by this mindset, you will grow in your relationship with God.

Lord, I believe . . .

_____

_____

_____

_____

_____

_____

_____

_____

_____

_____

_____

_____

_____

_____

February 25

"I don't refer to all of you when I tell you these things, for I know the ones I've chosen—to fulfill the Scripture that says, 'The one who shared supper with me treacherously betrays me.'"
(John 13:18 TPT)

Jesus chose His closest friends, the twelve disciples. They left jobs, families and the comfort of home to walk, minister and learn from Jesus. One of the chosen was Judas Iscariot, who would betray Him unto death. Jesus knew that. Jesus knew when He first laid eyes on Judas that he was the one who would betray Him. And yet He still chose Judas. He still taught him. He still sat at the table with him and washed his feet. We can learn from Jesus's relationship with Judas how to love those who hurt and betray us.

Lord, I believe . . .

_____

_____

_____

_____

_____

_____

_____

_____

_____

_____

February 26

> "Not so, my lord," Hannah replied, "I am a
> woman who is deeply troubled. I have not been
> drinking wine or beer; I was pouring out my soul
> to the LORD." (1 Samuel 1:15)

Hannah is accused of being drunk when she is actually pouring out her soul to the Lord. She longed for a child and was moved so deeply by her faith in God and His mighty power to work in her life that her emotions were perceived as drunkenness. When was the last time you felt so moved by the Spirit? What does pouring your soul out to the Lord look like?

Lord, I believe . . .

_____
_____
_____
_____
_____
_____
_____
_____
_____
_____
_____
_____
_____
_____

"As we grow in our understanding of God's character, may we also grow in the absolute truth that not one thing in this world can separate us from His love."

Tammy Trent

READ

TRUST

BELIEVE

February 27

For the kingdom of God is not a matter of eating and drinking, but of righteousness, peace and joy in the Holy Spirit. . . . (Romans 14:17)

Paul is talking about the concern of the law that many people still possess. Under the Old Testament law, there were many rules about what, where and when you were allowed to eat and drink. When Jesus came, He abolished the need for those laws. Paul explains that the Kingdom of God is no longer a place ruled by laws of eating and drinking but a place of righteousness and peace and joy! We have these things because of Jesus and because of the work of the Holy Spirit in our lives today.

Lord, I believe . . .

_____

_____

_____

_____

_____

_____

_____

_____

_____

_____

_____

_____

_____

February 27

For the kingdom of God is not a matter of eating and drinking, but of righteousness, peace and joy in the Holy Spirit. . . . (Romans 14:17)

Paul is talking about the concern of the law that many people still possess. Under the Old Testament law, there were many rules about what, where and when you were allowed to eat and drink. When Jesus came, He abolished the need for those laws. Paul explains that the Kingdom of God is no longer a place ruled by laws of eating and drinking but a place of righteousness and peace and joy! We have these things because of Jesus and because of the work of the Holy Spirit in our lives today.

Lord, I believe . . .

February 28

> *"Suppose one of you has a hundred sheep and loses one of them. Doesn't he leave the ninety-nine in the open country and go after the lost sheep until he finds it?"* (Luke 15:4)

Each one of us has immeasurable worth to God because we are created in His image. We are His precious children. You are loved as His son or daughter. Never allow yourself to think that you don't matter or that God doesn't love or care about you. God sees you, and He loves you today and every day. He leaves the flock to find you when you're lost.

Lord, I believe . . .

_____
_____
_____
_____
_____
_____
_____
_____
_____
_____
_____
_____
_____
_____